LELAND HOBURG

BLACKWUELFE@YAHOO.COM

BLACKWUELFE.HUBPAGES.COM

I0475437

INTERNATIONAL EXPANSION OF THE UNITED STATES RETAIL INDUSTRY INTO THE EUROPEAN MARKET

TABLE OF CONTENTS

TABLE OF CONTENTS 2

EXECUTIVE SUMMARY 3

PURPOSE 5

INTRODUCTION 7

PREPARATION TO EUROPE EXPANSION 11

OPERATING IN EUROPE 24

CHALLENGES TO EUROPEAN EXPANSION 46

CONCLUSION 64

REFERENCES 68

BIBLIOGRAPHY 70

EXECUTIVE SUMMARY

US retailers face problems in the area of domestic expansion, a mature market, and for some retailers, an oversaturated and highly competitive market place. Expansion into the European market for many retailers is the best option for continued growth.

Europe is a sophisticated and developed marketplace. The use of the Euro by most of the EU countries means companies expanding into Europe can centralize or regionalize their base of operations.

The US retailer must have a strategic plan. Expansion into the European market is not easy or without risks. The expansion process must fit within the company's ability to grow. The company's ability to expand into Europe is dependent upon their size (format) and financial strength.

International expansion is not easy. What a business does in the US may not translate well abroad. US large format retailers are changing the way European retailers do business and the shopping patterns of European consumers.

Companies will have to answer many questions before entering the European market. Companies will have to determine which country to enter first, the market entry strategy, the level of ownership, the adaptability of their systems, the necessary product reformulation and packaging changes, and business practices changes to accommodate EU and local governmental restrictions and requirements. Research is the key to any successful European expansion.

PURPOSE

The purpose of this book is to study the United States (US) retail industry in regards to international expansion into the European Union (EU) market including: the decision to expand internationally and the country or countries targeted for initial expansion; the differences in marketing practices between the US and EU markets for point of purchase marketing; the differences in product differentiation and product mix including formulation and product packaging regulations or requirements per country; the differences between US and European views on impulse items as opposed to shopping goods, and the differences in views towards "import goods" vs. "domestic goods" in Europe; the entry barriers US retailers' face including level of ownership, governmental regulations, and restrictions, and land usage regulations that limit the physical location of operations; and supply chain difficulties or advantages faced by US retailers in Europe.

INTRODUCTION

International expansion is not a new concept. McDonalds, Coke, and Pepsi have a successful record of international expansion. International expansion is not without trials and errors. Proper adjustments reflect new information from the errors. US retailers face problems in the area of domestic expansion, a mature market, and in certain sectors of the retail industry, an oversaturated and highly competitive market place. If a business can no longer expand in its home market where then is it to expand? US businesses do have several options: regional expansion close to US borders, i.e. Canada or Mexico; regional expansion within the Americas, i.e. Brazil, Peru, etc; or global expansion into another region or country around the globe.

The expansion process must fit within the company's ability to grow, meaning the company's internal support systems, physical structures, external suppliers, and personnel are in a position to handle the additional load created by the expansion. As a company expands, the expansion should be at an organic rate of growth not a forced rate of growth. An organic rate of growth means a company can only expand as rapidly as it has the ability to reinvest resources to further the expansion and maintain current operations. A forced rate of growth means a company is expanding beyond the current capabilities of its systems. Growth for many US companies means expanding internationally.

International expansion is not easy. What a business does in the US may not translate well abroad, because companies are not only exporting products, services, or practices, but also exporting American culture. In some cases, the exporting of American culture is detrimental to a company's success abroad, as is the case with Disney still struggling with Euro Disney of Paris. The quest for new sources of revenue often fuels the risk taking of expansion. Besides competition from domestic competitors, the US retailer also faces competition from foreign multinational retailers in the European market. Success at home may not mean success abroad as many European retailers have found out about the US market place. According to Simms (October 23, 2003), "The US has proved a graveyard for British retailers from Marks & Spencer to The Body Shop, which, seduced by the apparent similarities between US and UK consumers, were caught out by the significant differences."

Before US retailers enter the European market they have several questions to answer. Which country does the company enter first? Does the company tailor its business to local taste or use a "cookie cutter" approach? What level of ownership will the company have: franchises, joint ventures, or wholly owned subsidiaries? Will the company's internal support systems, supply chains or IT, be able to adapt or will it need new and different systems? How a company's operations have to change to accommodate governmental restrictions and requirements? What differences in packaging or product formulation will a company have to make? What adjustments to the product mix are necessary? Will the company's product(s) meet the expectations of the local consumer?

PREPARATION TO EUROPE EXPANSION

To establish a business in a new market requires research. Preparing for expansion should include the following: knowledge of the local situation, careful attention to detail, knowledge of local tastes and compliance to local codes, the transfer of knowledge and technical knowhow, and patience. One important consideration is the length of time a company expects operations to become profitable. Companies should not expect an immediate return on the investment. A few select countries, England and France primarily, do not use the Euro; with this in mind US retailers can view Western Europe as a homogeneous market from a monetary point of view. The question remains: how would a company choose which country to enter?

The results of a company's research of a potential market will generate key indicators of the local situation.

Key indicators include the size of the market, the GDP of country, the competition within industry sector, the growth potential, and the availability of potential workforce. Another factor is the legal environment in the target market country including the restrictions and regulations regarding general business practices, franchising, and labor relations. It is important to understand the restrictions and regulations on promotional activities, along with which media outlets to use, and language considerations. Research should uncover the availability of local suppliers, and the difficulties of establishing a local supply chain. The availability of real estate and regulations involving real estate planning and development is another key factor in an expansion process. It is important to know the local competition, know who they are and what they do best.

The basic facts about operating in Europe: the population density is higher than the US, the average delivery distances are shorter, the cost for fuel is higher, the delivery regulations vary by city and/or country, and many European countries have stricter labor regulations. Given the basic facts of operating in Europe all those factors may affect the profitability of the US retailer operating in Europe.

Most European countries have a higher population density than the US. For example, England is roughly the size of Oregon with a population near one-quarter of the US population, approximately 65 million. Germany has the greatest population of all the European countries with a population over eighty million. Germany, England (UK), France, and Italy combined roughly equate to the same size of population to the US.

The cost for fuel across the EU is higher for gasoline and diesel. The current US price per litre for gasoline averages around .45 US Dollars. In Europe, the range for fuel cost is from .45 US Dollars per litre of gasoline in Moldova to 1.23 US Dollars per litre of gasoline in Norway, with a similar range for diesel prices.

Due to denser populations and stricter real estate usage regulations, there are limited options for warehouses and distribution centers, coupled with many European cities have local statutes preventing night deliveries or Sunday deliveries. According to Gentry (September 2003), "One executive quoted in the Kurt Salmon report said his company is required to deliver within a limited 14-hour window to 40% of its stores. This stringent control forces the retailer to maintain a transportation fleet that is 20% larger than would be necessary if there were flexibility in timing."

Unlike the workaholic culture in the US, many EU countries have strict regulations on labor relations and labor practices limiting when and how long a person can work, Belgium, for example, had until recently limited the nighttime working hours of women to midnight with the exception of medical personnel and prostitutes. German lawmakers are considering limiting the workweek of hourly employees to a thirty-two hour workweek. In England, for example, businesses coordinate their holiday (vacation) time with the academic calendar, enabling families to have more leisure time together.

Other details that can make or break a business include institutional factors regarding regulations on competition, hours of operation, labor practices, and land-usage and real estate development.

Real estate development and land usage may make expansion into the European market difficult. The real estate market is certainly different from the US, according to Guy (2001), "Land and property markets which may be characterized by high prices, legal restrictions, or other idiosyncrasies." Land usage is a problem for many large format US firms heading into Europe, i.e. Wal-Mart and Warner Brothers Warner Village. Many European countries have regulations on the development of out-of-center (away from the town center or traditional retail areas) and limits to the size of the development. Hypermarkets, a large format store containing both a supermarket and department store under one roof, are between a supermarket and supercenter in size. Hypermarkets are the common large format store used throughout the EU. France, for example, over the last decade enacted laws effecting large format retailers. One law aimed at limiting German companies from expanding into France limited the number of large food retailers operating in France. For a large format retailer to enter the French marketplace they must purchase an existing retailer. In effect, the French hypermarket format marketplace is a closed system. To gain market share in the French hypermarket market a company must buy existing operations, and thus the number of stores remains the same, a zero sum gain for the market. Another law recently enacted in France, clearly aimed at US retailers by prohibiting loss leaders, favors the local supermarket. Retailers in other sectors, i.e. Food Service, may not have as many difficulties with land usage by choosing to locate in traditional retail areas.

Attention to the differences between domestic and non-domestic markets can be the difference between success and failure. Adjustments to the product or product mix to reflect local taste may be the edge for a company to be successful in expansion in the European market. Early expansion by US companies often carried the arrogance of the "Ugly American," meaning doing it the same way abroad as home, globalizing taste from a US point of view. Companies like McDonalds, Coke-Cola, Anheuser-Busch, and Pepsi benefited from economies of scale especially in the area of marketing. Eventually declining sales forced variations in the product and product mix to adjust for the consumers' tastes. Coke-Cola, for example, has over three hundred products, many to meet local taste. McDonalds, with its 30,000 international stores, learned over time to adjust for local tastes at home and abroad. Sometimes the competitive edge for a company comes in the form of its "American heritage." Roadhouse Grill, for example, is using its concept of an original American steak house with a western theme as a competitive advantage in the European restaurant market place.

The transfer of knowledge and technical knowhow is often closely tied to the level of ownership a company has in the new market. Ownership may be in the form of a merger or acquisition, a joint venture, a franchised operation, or licensed operation. Ownership is also contingent upon the target country of operations. Most EU countries allow wholly owned subsidiaries. Portugal, for example, limits ownership to fifty percent non-domestic ownership. When Roadhouse Grill looked to expand into the European market, in 2000, they entered into a joint venture with Cremonini, an Italian multifaceted foodservice concern. Roadhouse provides the concept and Cremonini contributes the knowledge of the European market. According to Battaglia (July 24, 2000), "Roadhouse Grill plans to bring Cremonini's foreign staffs to its US restaurants for initial training programs while also sending corporate support to Italy to help establish systems for restaurant, training and office operations." Roadhouse Grill as mentioned by Battaglia (2000) faces little competition in the casual dining chain restaurant marketplace throughout Europe. Roadhouse Grill strength lies in the emphasis on quality and value.

New markets take time to develop as many US multinationals discover. There are obstacles to growth besides the already present competition. Countries in Western Europe are mature markets, benefiting from the post World War II aid from the US for rebuilding. The former communist blocs, Eastern European countries, are developing markets due to the slow change from a socialist based market to a competitive market. Eastern European countries may require larger investments for the initial expansion phase of a company's expansion, especially in the area of infrastructure development and shipping.

Wal-Mart discovered an obstacle in the form of strict governmental regulations. Wal-Mart bought the Wertkauf chain in Germany in 1998 but growth in mainland Europe is slow due to regulations for building out-of-center retail outlets. Growth for Wal-Mart, in Germany, is also slow due to restrictions on pricing, store operation hours, and limits placed on land usage. In the United Kingdom, Wal-Mart purchased the Asda chain of 229 stores and faced similar problems. The share of Wal-Marts sales derived from non-domestic markets rose from 4.8% in 1997 to 14 % in 2000. Wal-Mart is using an investment strategy by buying existing operations to expand into the European market. According to Johnson (2000), on Wal-Marts market entry strategy, "Typically they commit to a region or territory making massive investments, even if it takes many years to get what we would call in the US good returns." Wal-Mart is taking the long-term approach of developing their infrastructure and gaining a foothold in a market over immediate returns on the investment. Wal-Mart is taking a slow and cautious approach. As with Wal-Marts expansion domestically, their European expansion has forced the competition to reevaluate their business practices.

A company, when exploring the option of international expansion into the European market, has many factors to consider. Once the proposed country or countries for expansion are thoroughly examined, a decision needs is to be made either to expand into the European market or not to expand into the European market. Expansion is a risk-taking venture. The quality of a company's research should minimize the risk and reduce the ambiguity associated with the target market. The research should aid the decision making process and indicate which country or market to enter. Based on upon population, legal environment for business operations, and other factors, Italy, England, or Germany are possible starting points for expansion for US retailers entering the EU market. England and Germany have a history of being proving grounds for US businesses operating in Europe and as launching points for the whole of Europe. Success in Germany and England's more stringent environments may translate to success throughout Europe. Italy, Germany, and England, also, have the largest populations of military service personnel, their families, and US expatriates in residence.

OPERATING IN EUROPE

After choosing the target country for initial expansion, a company needs to determine the nature of the expansion: What market entry strategy will be used to enter the market? What level of ownership will the company have; franchises, joint ventures, or wholly owned subsidiaries? Will the company tailor its business to local taste or will the company use a "cookie cutter" approach? Will logistics be a problem?

How a company enters a market is important. It will often determine the long-term success of the company's foreign ventures. There are basic strategies for a company to use when expanding internationally: an investment strategy, a multinational strategy, or a global strategy. An investment strategy is the purchasing existing operations. A multinational strategy is the development of fully or partially owned subsidiaries adapted to the local market. A global strategy is the use of similar operations domestically and internationally. A company's strategy for entering any market may depend on many factors including the ability to finance the expansion process adequately and not to the detriment of other operations. Some of the factors a company must consider when choosing a strategy for market entry include location of operations, size of operations, availability of suppliers or transportation cost, and the legal environment for general business practices. Expansion is a risk; to limit the risk a company must have a clearly defined plan for expansion. While it is easier for a company to open a store in Chicago than Budapest, the market entry strategy the retailer uses should allow the retailer to meet the local consumer's needs.

The nature of the operation influences the market entry strategy. As previously stated, the larger the retail space needed in Europe the harder it is to expand using a multinational strategy or global strategy. Large format retailers are often limited to an investment strategy. The use of the investment strategy is due to population density and land usage regulations. Smaller retailers, meaning those needing less space, may find either a multinational or a global strategy adequate for their expansion purposes. Companies that are successful globally take an integrated approach to international expansion, according to Nannery (1999), "They've included every element of their business working in unison."

There are technological barriers to international expansion retailers should not dismiss. Technological preparedness is important. Point-of-sales (POS) systems used domestically may not adapt well to the target market for a variety of reasons including taxation and language specifications. From the IT viewpoint, a company must adapt current systems or use new systems to provide the support the business needs as it grows internationally. Talbots, for example, customized their POS package with built in programming to handle the various taxation and language specifications for their foreign operations. Talbot's system allows them to make buying and merchandising decisions from the US. In this case, if a consumer walked into a Talbots store in London they would see similar merchandise also found in a store in Chicago. Reebok used a different approach with their franchised stores in Europe. Currently the owner-operators run the businesses with the help of an adaptable software package from Retail Pro. Even though Reebok concedes that the Retail Pro package will not meet their future needs, it allows them to open a store in a matter of months, thus giving them time to adapt their current systems to meet future needs. Whatever the approach a company chooses for their system needs, it must be able to support all aspects of operating a business in a foreign country.

The logistical barriers of international expansion include managing the logistics of intercontinental expansion, adapting to the logistical complexities of the target market, and complying with the regulatory environment. Another decision many companies face is the method of moving inventories and supplies. The question is Does a company use and expand its own systems or contract with a third party logistics (3PL) firm, i.e. UPS or Fed Ex? Many European countries have social contracts with workers at every level of society, making it difficult to develop the flexibility with logistics that firms enjoy in the US. Many European cities have local statutes preventing night deliveries or Sunday deliveries, coupled with higher fuel cost and land use regulations. The best option for a smaller company is to contract with a 3PL firm. Larger companies like Wal-Mart and Costco may want to develop their own delivery fleets. According to Trunick (June 2003), "Logistics executives want the 3PL operation to turn logistics cost into a variable cost and also be very adaptable."

One logistical problem currently facing US retailers in the European market is the variety of packaging and labeling requirements that vary from country to country. Even though the European Congress is working to standardize regulations across its member states, the larger issue is the use of disposable or one-way packaging. Europeans are for the most part are more environmentally conscience then their US counterparts. The use of a recyclable packaging is environmentally appealing. In the beverage industry in Europe the use of recyclable packaging is a controversial issue. Alcoholic beverages and juices are typically sold in one-way packages across most of Europe while non-alcoholic beverages (CDS) and mineral waters are typically sold in returnable containers. In many of the returnable markets, standardized bottles are primarily used. From a marketing point of view, standardization makes it harder achieve product uniqueness through the shape or the color of the bottle, i.e. Coke-Cola's contour bottle or 7 Up's green bottle. Many European countries are regulating towards the use of returnable packaging to encourage recycling and reduce the amount of trash produced. Aldi, a hard discounter grocery chain, primarily uses only one-way packaging for their products in the European market. For example, in Germany, hard discounters account for nearly half of the supermarket sales, yet most Germans purchase beer and CDS's for offsite consumption from other sources. Since Germans purchase beer and CDS's from other source than the supermarket, this in effect reduces cross merchandising advantages and impulse shopping opportunities and sales. The logistical cost of using returnable packaging includes the handling, sorting, and storing of the returnable package. It is understandable that the additional cost associated with returnable packaging can be an entry barrier into the market.

Retailers in the food service industry often "manufacture" their product(s) on site, which eliminates the logistical complexities of packaging and transporting products to Europe. The problem these retailers face is finding reliable providers for raw materials. The raw materials may differ from their US counterparts due to the EU's list of banned coloring agents and preservatives. Will a Krispy Kreme doughnut taste the same in Munich as it does in Davenport? The competitive edge in the food service industry is the consistency of the product, as well as, the theme. Researching potential and reliable providers is important to the success of the operation. The future success for the food and beverage industry and the food service industry lies in the increasing numbers of US expatriates living in Europe and the increasing number of Europeans working or studying in the US. These are people looking for a taste of home or the taste of something acquired abroad.

Which approach retailers use to their European operations, a "cookie cutter" approach, or multinational approach, is vital to their success. A multinational approach is varying the stores appearance, product mix, product formulation, or product packaging for different localities. A "cookie cutter" approach is doing everything the same regardless of the location. How will all of the company's stores look? Will the stores look the same, or will they vary from locale to locale? If a company uses franchisors, how much control will the company have over their operations? Control of franchised operations is a domestic problem US retailers are used to facing in the US. Many franchise agreements clearly define the rights and duties of all parties involved. Internationally, franchising laws vary from country to country. England, for example, does not have any specific legislation regarding franchise operations. England relies upon the British Franchise Association and the European Franchise Federation to oversee franchisors and franchisees. Both organizations have voluntary codes of ethics for their members to follow. The British Franchise

Association requires its members to go through a stringent accreditation process. The aim of the accreditation process is to increase industry standards and raise the quality of franchisors.

With franchising in Europe, US retailers face the same dilemma they do when franchising in US. The question is how to choose the franchisee. The company can look for another company as the master franchisor that sets the business as a wholly owned subsidiary or for an individual that has the capital and successful record of accomplishment in team building and business operations. For the US retailer, the solution requires careful research of the potential business partners and a clear set of requirements.

The challenge in building a multinational or global brand is to maintain consistency of the brand or brand image. The level of control over any joint or franchised operations in the European market affects consistency. It is important to understand the laws of the target market country regarding the franchise agreement. The franchise agreement is the key to maintaining consistency of the brand. The agreement outlines the general business practices for the franchised operations ensuring the consistency of the brand and brand image. The franchise agreement should clearly outline the responsibilities, duties, and possible penalties for both the franchisor and franchisee. The franchise agreement is the tool which the franchisor maintains control over the product, brand name, or brand image. The more control a company has over its image and products the more consistent the image and products are across the varying markets. McDonalds, over the years, experienced what happens when a company does not do enough research before entering a market. Like many early explorers if they survived, they learned from their mistakes.

Degradation of the brand image occurs when a company does not retain control over its product or name. Companies often risk losing sales and the inability to fuel further expansion when they do not maintain control over their product or image in their franchised operations. Brand names and products relate to a set of preconceived assumptions in the mind of the consumer. The preconceived assumptions often relate to the intrinsic ideals of quality, value, reliability, etc. For most companies, the images their products create in the mind of the consumer are as important as the products themselves.

Building a global or multinational brand also requires developing a global or multinational campaign. According to Miller (2002), "Merchandising and display lends itself to international branding because it is marketing without languages." A point of purchase (POP) display is an easy way to generate sales through impulse purchases. Developing a multinational or global POP campaign requires research, simplicity, and consistency. Do the necessary research to understand the different markets and cross-cultural practicalities of the POP campaign. Simplicity means to create a basic template that is adaptable to the local market and keeping the designs and wording simple. Marketers must understand what works in one market may not work in other markets. In France, for example, many of the hypermarkets use dump bins at the end of aisles, which may not work well for a smaller retailer found in England.

There are some challenges in building multinational POP campaigns. Some markets are more restrictive. Germany, for example, has comprehensive laws regarding recycling which may restrict the materials used for the display. Another example, in England, the marketer may need to develop multiple POP displays for one campaign to meet the restrictions of individual retail chains. Even though brand consistency is the goal, there are practical reasons for the adaptability of the POP campaign, the differences in markets. Consistency of the message across the different markets is important. Marketers must understand that the era of the global retailer and the global shopper has arrived.

Retailers have gone global through the internet, and by expanding into Europe, and the shopper has gone global using the internet. Yahoo!, an internet domain company and service provider, has domains tailored by locality, by country, and by multinational region. A shopper can easily visit any domain Yahoo! provides with a click of the mouse.

Another challenge in building a multinational or global brand relates to how the product will look, feel, or taste as compared to the product produced and sold in the US. This is a challenge for the food and beverage industry as well as the restaurant segment. The EU bans some of the preservatives, colorings, and other additives commonly found in food products produced in the US. An example of a banned additive is benzoic acid, found naturally in US grown cranberries, occurs in high enough levels to be listed as an additive for the labeling standards in a few European countries. Spain is one country requiring a complete listing of all ingredients, including ingredients that naturally occur in the product. Food purity laws differ from country to country but the EU congress is trying to standardize regulations across its member states. Another example, in Germany, beer can only be brewed using four ingredients: yeast, water, hops, and malt. Food purity laws also extend to how products are classified or named. In the EU for a wine to be a Champaign, it must come from a specific grape and grown in the Champaign region of France. Otherwise, a similar product not from the Champaign region of France is labeled as a naturally fermented sparkling wine. For large format retailers, Wal-Mart and Costco, for example, how their products are labeled on the shelves is important. Labeling standards must be met to avoid fines and other penalties.

As with all food products taste is important. Accommodating the differences in regional/country preferences can make a difference. McDonalds, Pepsi, and Coke are three examples of reformulating and customizing offerings of their products to fit the taste of the host country/region. Reformulation of the product requires careful research that includes researching potential suppliers for ingredients. Many carbonated beverages (flavored sodas/CDS's) produced in Europe use sugar as the sweetening agent as opposed to corn syrup that is primarily used in North America. Sugar is readily available in Europe and is less expensive than the corn syrup that is primarily produced in the US. Flavoring agents and other additives are strictly regulated by the EU. Changing the formulation of a product can possibly change the appearance, taste, and texture of the product from its US origins.

Along with the taste and the appearance of the product, the product packaging is important for a successful expansion. In the beverage industry, product packaging regulations and local requirements can be entry barriers in markets requiring the use of recyclable packaging. Markets using recyclable packaging for beverages often use a common bottle to ease handling cost. The common bottle is usually a clear plastic bottle designed to accommodate a variety of CDS's, water, and fruit juices. For the local bottler a common bottle lowers cost by reducing the variety of bottles required for various products. A common bottle creates a problem for the marketer. The problem for the marketer is distinguishing their product from other products visually. Coca Cola's distinctive bottle is as important as the taste in separating Coke from other colas.

The restaurant segment of the retail industry has the greatest potential for expansion in the EU market. Even though Europeans are used to the McDonalds, Burger Kings, Pizza Huts, etc. the "fast food" segment of the restaurant business; casual dining themed restaurants are crossing the pond to Europe. There is a lack of competition in the casual dining segment across Europe. The idea of casual dining themed restaurants is new to Europeans. For many Europeans the "eat, drink, and be yourself" concept of dining provides a unique dining experience especially in a uniquely "American" themed restaurant. Applebee's and Roadhouse Grill, for example, are bringing casual dining and distinctly "American" themed restaurants to Europe. Currently Roadhouse Grill operates four stores in Italy and Applebee's operates five stores in Greece with future openings, for 2005 in England and Germany. Hippopotamus and Buffalo Grill are the local competition in France but both have been slow to expand beyond France.

Expansion requires a strategic plan with clearly defined goals, operational objectives, and a timetable for meeting those goals and objectives. The timetable for meeting the goals and the objectives must be an important part of a company's plan. An example is Roadhouse Grill's expansion into the European market through a joint venture with Cremonini. Both companies are essentially providing half of the technical expertise for a successful operation. Roadhouse Grill provides the tactical and technical knowledge of operating a themed restaurant with an American Old West theme. Cremonini provides the knowledge of the target market, the available suppliers, and how to adapt Roadhouse Grill to meet the expectations of the Italian restaurant guest.

It is evident that expansion is a risk-taking venture requiring several elements for a successful expansion. The key to any decision regarding international expansion is research. Fully understanding the situation in the target market, reducing the level of ambiguity, and other risk factors is why research is important. Once the research phase is completed, a company can develop a strategic plan for the expansion process. The strategic plan is a set of goals and a timetable to meet those goals. The goals in the strategic plan should reflect the company's overall strategic plan for business.

CHALLENGES TO EUROPEAN EXPANSION

The EU European Congress is working towards commonality of many laws across its member states. The laws cover a variety of topics including general business practices, import tariffs and taxation, and social-political issues. The EU replaced the North America as the largest trading zone. The EU draws over twenty percent of the products produced worldwide; while currently nineteen to twenty percent of the products produced worldwide go to North America. The EU is looking toward continued growth in the number of member states. Currently seven countries are applying for EU membership.

With the exception of England, Denmark, and Sweden, the EU is a single currency zone. The use of the Euro reduces the redundancy of accounting systems needed to operate in multiple countries in Europe. The approach for many smaller retailers (in size of space needed) to expand into the EU is no different from the approach they would take in the US. Large format retailers do have a different set of obstacles to overcome, many relating to land usage laws and out-of-center zone laws.

US large format retailers realistically have only one option available to them for expansion into EU countries. The large format retailers must use an investment strategy as their market entry strategy due the land usage laws most EU countries of Western Europe currently enforce to limit out-of-center shopping zones. Using an investment strategy sounds easy. Just purchase a chain in the target market, convert the stores in the chain into X-Mart company stores, and as the revenues increase from the European expansion, the X-

Mart company continues to grow organically and takeover other companies in other markets.

It sounds easy for companies to acquire additional revenue through acquisitions and then continue to grow with each additional acquisition. The challenge is not only to acquire revenue dollars, but, also, to acquire profit dollars. Profit dollars are harder to obtain. Companies must be wary of the "White Elephant" syndrome. What may look good on paper may end up being cumbersome to operate and difficult to integrate into the company. Companies using the investment strategy must consider how to acquire companies that will easily fit within the corporate strategic plan, how to convert the acquisition to the company store profile, how the acquisition will provide the company with revenue dollars and profit dollars, and how the acquisition will provide the company with a strong market presence.

The profit dollars are not to be short-term gains but gains made by developing the potential of the acquisition. The primary challenges to US large format retailers will be to find companies to acquire, to integrate the acquisition into the company, and to create global efficiencies with the acquired companies.

As discussed earlier, Italy, England, and Germany are possible starting points for international expansion. The markets in Italy, England, and Germany could quickly become oversaturated by US retailers entering the market. For a US retailer, the competition may not be from a company from the target market country but from another US based company. Knowing the competition in the target market and knowing which companies are targeting the same market is essential. Due to the higher population density of many European countries, the potential consumers in any given area are similar to the market of a larger US metropolitan area. Companies entering the EU market need to approach the expansion as they would a domestic expansion into a primarily urban market. Urban markets typically have limited areas available for real estate development and warehousing, stricter zoning and land usage laws, and availability of a potential workforce.

As previously stated, many EU countries have strict regulations on labor relations and labor practices, often limiting when and how long a person can work. This is unlike the work culture in the US. Europeans have more leisure time compared to their US counterparts. More leisure time relates directly to the differences of shopping patterns between shoppers in the US and shoppers in most EU countries. Europeans tend to shop for food products more often than shoppers in the US do. With the expansion of US large format retailers into Europe, Europeans shopping patterns are starting to change.

Shopping patterns in Germany, for example, show consumers shop at a supermarket or hypermarket for most foodstuffs and juices, another establishment for offsite consumption of alcoholic beverages and CDS's, and another for the bakery products. Another example is from Paris, France, there are one-hundred-eight independent bakeries scattered throughout the city (excluding the larger metropolitan area). The population of Paris, France is approximately two million while the total metropolitan area has a population of approximately nine and a half million. Paris, France is similar in size by population to Houston, Texas while the total metropolitan area for Paris, France is similar in size by population to the Chicago, Illinois Metropolitan Area. This is much smaller than New York, New York (approximately nine million) or its metropolitan area (twenty-one million) supports only fifty independent bakeries within the city itself. This reflects the shopping patterns of the US consumers, typically buying food products during weekly trips to the supermarket or the supercenter.

European shopping patterns for items other than food products have slowly changed over the last twenty years. The development of large format retailers in Europe is partially accountable for the changing shopping patterns, along with the expansion of large format retailers from the US entering the market. IKEA, a Swedish large format houseware retailer, has helped change how many Europeans shop for furniture and other household items. Instead of visiting a variety of shops for furniture and lighting needs, the shopper can now visit an IKEA store, which offers multiple styles all under one roof.

Traditional European shopping patterns for shopping goods meant visiting a variety of specialized merchants in a centralized retail district. The retail districts were often located in areas of the city that once were the cities markets. Some districts may be located in a "downtown" area or in the town square. With the development of the large format retailers in Europe, shopping began to move away from the traditional retail districts. The late 1960's and 1970's saw a boom period for the development of the hypermarket store format in Europe. The hypermarket boom fueled the move away from traditional retail areas. The hypermarket boom was partially due to the looser land usage and zoning regulations of the period. Many European countries reacted to the move away from traditional areas by enacting laws limiting out-of-center retail development and the development of the large format retailer. While some US large format retailers are bringing their distinctive style to European shoppers, other US retailers are tailoring their style to meet the demands of the culture and to take advantage of the traditional shopping patterns.

US retailers like Ethan Allen and Office Depot are taking advantage of the traditional European shopping pattern. Ethan Allen and Office Depot offer multiple services under one roof but these services are all part of one category, i.e. office supplies or furniture. According to Prior (2002), Office Depot expects that less than half of its revenue will come from its North American operations. Office Depot and Ethan Allen are successful in the US, where the market is saturated, but must expand internationally to continue to grow. Ethan

Allen's success in Europe, according to Sheridan (2000), is due to their product designs and their emphasis on customer service. The shopper in Europe expects more in the way of customer service while the US shopper is accustom to the "serve yourself" concept for large format retailers.

The expansion of US large format retailers affects the European shopping patterns. A Wal-Mart Supercenter, for example, is multiple "stores" under one roof, a pharmacy, a clothing retailer, a hardware store, an electronics store, etc. Wal-Marts expansion into Europe is affecting how Europeans shop. In Germany, for example, according to Johnson (2000), "Wal-Mart has already had a tremendous impact on food retailing. Wal-Mart has cut prices, introduced its customary service, and greeters at the door." Wal-Mart expanded into Germany through the purchase of the German hypermarket chains of Wertkauf and Interspar. According to Guy (2001), Wal-Mart was able to increase retail presentation space within a converted Wertkauf hypermarket, in Dortmund, Germany by nearly two-thousand cubic meters, add specialty areas, and add an extra sixty-two personnel to the staff. As seen in the US, the supercenter creates a one-stop shopping experience, with a variety of products and services under one roof. Companies like Wal-Mart, Target, and Costco are converting the acquired hypermarkets to resemble supercenters. Even though US large format retailers do have challenges in their expansion into the EU markets, their biggest impact in retailing in Europe is on food retailing.

US food retailers, grocery store chains, are avoiding Europe due to the highly competitive market. The European grocery market for is more consolidated than the US market which is characterized by many regional grocery chains and a few national chains. Due to the consolidation, European food retailers according to Harrison (1999) are able to have a net margin of three percent to five percent whereas US food retailers average around one percent in US. US food retailers are expanding internationally, just not in Europe where there are already strong competitors. Hybrid chains of food and general merchandise retailers like Wal-Mart and Costco are able to compete in the European food retail market. The hybrid chains offer more than just foodstuffs to the consumer.

A Wal-Mart Supercenter is an example of a hybrid store. Wal-Marts success at home and abroad is due to the productivity loop and through their use of technology. The productivity loop is the relationship between sales per square foot and overall profitability.

According to Johnson (2000), average sales per square foot of similarly sized Wal-Mart, K-Mart, and Target stores are as follows: Wal-Mart $413, K-Mart $222, and Target $253. Another part of the productivity loop is the use of private label brand merchandise, a company's store brand version of name brand items. The key to success with private label brand items is meeting the expectations of the customer, at a lower price than a similar major label brand item, this will ensure that the customer will likely to return and continue to purchase the private label brand. By using private label merchandise companies are able to generate repeat sales and build customer loyalty.

Wal-Marts use of technology for data warehousing, supply chain management and inventory management is also part of their success. Through data warehousing, Wal-Mart is able to reevaluate inventory needs, respond to changing demand patterns, and move merchandise from location to location as needed. According to Johnson (2000), "Wal-Mart is truly leading edge, when it comes to these sort of things, far beyond what major European retailers currently do."

US retailers will have other impacts upon the shopping patterns of Europeans. Traditionally European retailers do not carry a consistent range of products in the way US retailers do. One impact is the growing indifference to a preference to either foreign or domestic goods. Retailers are demanding better products at lower cost from the manufacturer. In turn, the manufacturers are meeting those demands. Suppliers, like Proctor & Gamble (P&G), are worldwide producers for a variety of fast moving products sold through large format retailers like Wal-Mart and Costco.

Retailers like Wal-Mart and Costco are trying to be the outlet through which P&G products are distributed throughout Europe, going to market by company instead of by country. With the EU, creating common standards for packaging across its member states, it will be making it easier and less costly for the multinational producer to distribute through one retail chain throughout Europe rather than one retail chain for each country. By creating a close relationship between the supplier and the retailer, the supplier is helping to lower cost for both. The cost savings for the supplier and the retailer are often in the area of transportation and handling cost. The supplier delivers to a centralized location instead of each individual store. The retailer is able to distribute the inventory as needed to meet product demand.

Retailers in Europe are taking notice of the US "invasion." European retailers have to reevaluate their business practices. European consumers' expectations are changing. The changes are due to the influx of retailers from the US. For the European retailer, it can no longer be business as usual and expect the local shopper to remain loyal to their retail outlets. As discussed earlier, US retailers often maintain a consistent mix of products. The consistent mix of products relates to building shopper loyalty and to the long-term success of the company through repeat sales.

European views on shopping goods and impulse items are quite similar to their US counterparts. Shopping goods often require some research by the consumer, often for the best features (in the mind of the purchaser), the best price, the availability of the product, etc. US retailers by being more consistent with their product mix than their European counterparts are enticing the European consumer to shop and to be repeat shoppers. For impulse items, the POP display is important, creating an unrecognized need in the mind of the consumer. Multinational promotional activities and global branding are influencing the way shoppers purchase. European consumers are acclimating to US retailers. The environment in which a consumer shops influences their purchasing decisions, if a shopper has to spend too much time searching for items then they are unlikely revisit. The easier it is to find merchandise and to offer a consistent mix of products creates a better shopping experience is for the consumer.

With many US markets already oversaturated the only way for US retailers to continue to grow is to expand internationally. US retailers are being lured by the prospect of the millions of consumers in the untapped markets around the globe. Europe is one of the major

untapped markets. Shoppers have gone global, brands

have gone global, and now retailers are going global.

CONCLUSION

In conclusion, US retailers face problems in the area of domestic expansion, a mature market, and in certain sectors of the retail industry, an oversaturated and highly competitive market place. Expansion into the European market for many retailers is the best option for continued growth. Europe is a sophisticated and developed marketplace. The use of the Euro by most of the EU countries means companies expanding into Europe can centralize or regionalize their base of operations.

Expansion into the European market is not easy or without risks. In the last five years, many US retailers are following the footsteps of McDonalds and other fast food retailers by invading the European landscape. US large format retailers are overcoming some of the challenges and restrictions placed upon land usage. Smaller format retailers are finding their niche in the European market place.

The expansion process must fit within the company's ability to grow. The company's ability to expand into Europe is dependent upon their size (format) and financial strength. International expansion is not easy. What a business does in the US may not translate well abroad. The quest for new sources of revenue often fuels the risk taking of expansion.

Besides competition from domestic competitors, the US retailer also faces competition from foreign multinational retailers in the European market. Wal-Mart, primarily, and other large format retailers are having a big impact on retailing in Europe. US large format retailers are changing the way European retailers do business. US large format retailers are changing the shopping patterns of Europeans with the introduction of hybrid stores to Europe, offering the consistency of products, and the better use of technology for merchandizing. US food service retailers are introducing to European restaurant landscape the concept of casual dining themed restaurants.

Companies will have to answer many questions before entering the European market. Companies will have to determine which country to enter first, the market entry strategy, the level of ownership, the adaptability of their systems, the necessary product reformulation and packaging changes, and business practices changes to accommodate EU and local governmental restrictions and requirements. Research is the key to any successful European expansion. US retailer must have a strategic plan that starts with a research phase. International expansion is not without trials and errors but research can minimize the errors

and reduce the associated risks.

REFERENCES

Battaglia, A. (July 24, 2000). Roadhouse Grill to move into Europe, inks joint pack with Cremonini. *Nation's Restaurant News 34, no 30.* p. 8.

Gentry, C. (September 2003). Continental divides. *Chain Store Age 79, no 9.* p. 70.

Guy, C. (2001). Internationalization of large-format retailers and leisure providers in Western Europe: Planning and property impacts. *International Journal of Retail & Distribution Management 29, no 10.* p. 452-461

Harrison, D. (July 1999). Food chains shun complex European market. *Frozen Food Age v47n12.* p. 26.

Johnson, J. (April 2000). The power broker. *Discount Merchandiser 40, no. 4.* p. 31-38.

Johnson, J. (April 2000). Expect the world from Wal-Mart. *Discount Merchandiser 40, no. 4.* p. 54

Miller, R. (August 8, 2002). How to exploit POP around the globe. *Marketing.* p. 27.

Nannery, M. (September 1999). Braving new worlds. *Chain Store Age 75, no. 9.* p. 69-74.

Prior, M. (May 20, 2002). Office Depot launches services in Italy. *Dsn Retailing Today 41, no 10.* p. 4, 56.

Sheridan, M. (February 2000). American merchants scout global shores. *Shopping Center World v29, no 2.* p. 84-85,115

Simms, J. (October 23, 2003). Travellers' tales.

Marketing. p. 37

Trunick, P. (June 2003). Flex Your Global Supply Chain. *Transportation & Distribution 44 no6.* p. 16, 18-19

BIBLIOGRAPHY

Anonymous. (March/April 2002). Logistics in the European Union. *Training Strategies for Tomorrow 16, no 2.* p. 10-12.

Anonymous. (September 2002). Success amid the gloom. *Europe (European Economic Community) no 419.* p. 34-45.

Anonymous. (March 2001). Think globally, act appropriately. *Progressive Grocer.* p. 21-26.

Anonymous. (October 1999). Expansion paradigm drives growth. *Discount Store News (Wal-Mart: Retailer of the Century Supplement).* p. 81, 177.

Bainbridge, J. (November 27, 2003). Disney magic has yet to take hold in Europe. *Marketing.* p. 15.

Battaglia, A. (July 24, 2000). Roadhouse Grill to move into Europe, inks joint pack with Cremonini. *Nation's Restaurant News 34, no 30.* p. 8.

Boylan, B. (November 13, 2000). Becoming a Household name on a global stage. *Crain's Chicago Business 23 no 47* p. 1, 73.

Crosby, L., & Johnson, S. (March/April 2002). The Globalization of relationship marketing. *Marketing Management 11, no 2.* p. 10-11.

Dignam, C. (January 2002). Welcome to euroland. *Ad Age Global 2, no 51.* p. 12.

Duckett, B. (May/June 2001). United Kingdom: Launching pad to European expansion. *Franchising World 33, no. 4.* p. 50-51.

Duff, M. (November 11, 2002). Continent's retail experts ask: Are hypermarket's days numbered? *DSN Retailing Today 41, no. 21.* p. 8.

Gentry, C. (September 2003). Continental divides. *Chain Store Age 79, no 9.* p. 70.

Groeber, J. (November 2002). A new frontier. *National Real Estate Investor 44, no 11.* p. 27-31.

Guy, C. (2001). Internationalization of large-format retailers and leisure providers in Western Europe: Planning and property impacts. *International Journal of Retail & Distribution Management 29, no 10.* p. 452-461.

Harris, T. (Writer), & Brady, W. (Director). (April 4, 2004). Knead to Know (The Bakeries of Paris, France). In E. Popkin (Producer), CBS News Sunday Morning Edition. New York, NY: CBS

Harrison, D. (July 1999). Food chains shun complex European market. *Frozen Food Age v47n12.* p. 26.

Howell, D. (November 11, 2002). Tapping markets home and abroad. *DSN Retailing Today 41, no. 21.* p. A11, A14.

Johnson, J. (April 2000). The power broker. *Discount Merchandiser 40, no. 4.* p. 31-38.

Johnson, J. (April 2000). Expect the world from Wal-Mart. *Discount Merchandiser 40, no. 4.* p. 54

Lisanti, T. (May 3, 1999). Europe's abuzz over Wal-Mart. *Discount Store News v38n9.* p. 11.

Metschies, G. (May 2003). International Fuel Prices. *International Fuel Prices, 3rd Edition.* Retrieved on February 3, 2004, from http://zietlow.com/docs/Fuel-Prices-2003.pdf

Miller, R. (August 8, 2002). How to exploit POP around the globe. *Marketing.* p. 27.

Miller, R. (May 24, 2001). Promotions aim to cross borders. *Marketing.* p. 31-32.

Nannery, M. (September 1999). Braving new worlds. *Chain Store Age 75, no. 9.* p. 69-74.

Prior, M. (May 20, 2002). Office Depot launches services in Italy. *Dsn Retailing Today 41, no 10.* p. 4, 56.

Ronning, J. (April 1999). Understanding Wal-Mart. *Discount Merchandiser v39n4.* p. 48-50.

Sheridan, M. (February 2000). American merchants scout global shores. *Shopping Center World v29, no 2.* p. 84-85,115

Simms, J. (October 23, 2003). Travellers' tales. *Marketing.* p. 37

Smith, G. (November/December 1999). Some things old-some things new. *Franchising World 31, no. 6.* p. 12-17

Soria, B. (April 2002). How to grow globally, despite a dismal economy. *Franchising World 34, no. 3.* p. 19-21

Troy, M. (July 12, 1999). Wal-Mart rocks European retailing as it rolls into United Kingdom. *Discount Store News v38n13.* p. 1, 81.

Troy, M. (June 4, 2001). Wal*Mart: From big to bigger: Stage is set for expansion. *Dsn Retailing Today 40, no. 11.* p. 60-63

Trunick, P. (June 2003). Flex Your Global Supply Chain. *Transportation & Distribution 44 no6.* p. 16, 18-19

Vida, I., Reardon, J., and Fairhurst, A. (2000). Determinants of international retail involvement: The case of large US retail chains. *Journal of International Marketing 8, no. 4.* p. 37-60.

Vuyk, C. (June 15, 2003). A balancing act in European packaging. *Beverage World v122, no. 1727.* p. 58.